this journal belongs to:

____

____

Welcome Friend!
to the Anchoring Amidst Journal,

This is the Anchoring Amidst Journal, because the resilience & confidence you're seeking is already in you. We're just here to give it space to rise.

The best part?! You ARE here. You made it. *You opened the pages to a journal that challenged you to call out your innermost tender - yet fortifying - trait.* Your resilience.

My deepest, truest wish for you is to turn each page knowing you are loved, whole, free and most importantly, yourself. Knowing that you can take what you learn here and apply right away.
Every single day. Every prompt. Every page.
Every opening. Every reconnection.

Here, you start from strength. Because that's what you have. Strength. Confidence. Resilience. Fulfillment.

The anchors we are building here are founded on 6 wholesome pillars.

Rooted in your beliefs.
Affirmed by your new narrative.
Slowed to see the beauty around you.
Reminded of where you are coming from
   * and where you're headed.
Gracious in your pursuit.
Held by your intentional thoughts and actions.

All of which we gently bring forth every week as we move through these daily prompts.

One by one, slowly washing resilience & confidence through our veins onto paper. Where it belongs. Strong. Intentional. Right. Because it's right now.
And that's all it needs to be.

In these pages you will find that you were never missing. Maybe just a little undiscovered. Maybe a little repressed. But never missing. Never alone. Never forgotten. Never more held than you are when you take this time to gently, rhythmically and methodically return to who God made you to be. You.

As you move through these prompts and pages. Take your time. Not all your answers will be clear or ready to be seen. But they are right. Because they are yours. And they are here. Waiting for you.
Just write. No judgement. No rules.

Two things you should know going into this journal:

First. This is yours. You won't see any more guidance from me between here and my closing letter… unless you want it. You can join me in the weekly ISO Prosperity Sisterhood conversations or by signing up for my email notes on my website. www.ShainaHargens.com - I look forward to walking this with you, however you choose.

Second. This journal was designed for women. The cycling, majestic, rhythmic beings that we are. It's for your WHOLE-NESS. This means that as the pages turn, every week is marked *1* through *4*. *Week *4* is written for your low confidence week - around your cycle week.*
If that's you right now, start there - skip ahead - you aren't missing anything you don't need right now. I promise.

XOXO
Shaina

psst... I left you some blank pages for all those things that are taking up space in your head. May you find the words, write them and do with them what you need to.
Sometimes we just need to write it OUT to feel our way THROUGH something. I got you. You got this. XOXO

Opening Check-In: Start From Here

How do I *honestly* feel today... physically, emotionally, spiritually?

What's been taking up the most space in my mind or heart lately?

What feels like it's missing... or quietly asking for my attention?

You may not know exactly what you want yet—but there are clues in what you miss, what you're drawn to, and what you daydream about.

One thing I deeply crave right now:

One part of me I want to reconnect with:

One small win I'd love to experience in the next 12 weeks:

This is the season where I ...

You're Already In Motion, XOXO

Just by opening these pages, you've taken the first step back toward your voice, your vision, and your peace. You don't need a master plan. You just need to find a rhythm—with yourself. Let's begin. XOXO

**"When you do things from your soul, you feel a
river moving in you, a joy." — Rumi**

What experience or moment this week made me feel truly fulfilled?

What 3 beliefs do I hold about myself that feel true today?

What value or belief of mine could I live out more fully this week?

***1* Fulfillment & Self-Awareness**

What is my heart or body quietly whispering (not shouting) to me?

What achievement deserves more recognition than I gave it?

What 3 chaotic things have I chosen lately & why?

I honor what fulfills me—and I move toward it with trust.

"You are altogether beautiful, my darling; there is no flaw in you." — Song of Solomon 4:7

What memory or thought is still warming my heart?

What does God say about me and how can I receive that truth?

What boundary / rule have I recently upheld, how did it serve me?

What 3 things do I crave more of in my daily life?

What personal identity stays steady, even when it all feels shaky?

What's stretching me right now & what is it making space for?

I am steady, even when life stretches me.

"Gratitude turns what we have into enough."
— Aesop

Where am I feeling the most gratitude right now?

What mantra or phrase has been on repeat in my mind lately?

What belief do I want to practice with more intention this week?

What 3 things am I doing to support my spiritual health?

What recent experience made me feel proud or accomplished?

When did I feel most "at home" this week & why or how?

I am grounded in grace and growing in purpose.

"Almost everything will work again if you unplug it for a few minutes... including you." — Anne Lamott

What moment made me feel deeply connected this week?

What affirmation or mantra feels especially true for me right now?

What personal rule or rhythm can I follow to create calm?

What part of me feels tired, tight, or tender & what helps soothe it?

What can I celebrate today, big or small?

What moment recently made me feel fulfilled?

Rest is not a reward—it's a rhythm I deserve.

"Confidence is the most beautiful thing you can wear." — Blake Lively

What feeling have I experienced that I'd love to feel more often?

What part of my identity feels grounded and unshakable?

What "no" did I say recently that made space for something better?

***1* Confidence & Clarity**

What 3 things am I doing for my physical or mental health?

If describing a recent accomplishment in juicy detail, what would I say?

What's stretching me & what strength is it building in me?

I am clear, capable, and becoming.

When did I feel most at peace & what was happening around me?

What are 3 things I'd love to see more of in the world?

What boundary or "no" helped me stay aligned with what matters?

What part of me feels worn out & what would replenish it?

What's something I handled recently that shows how far I've come?

What simple action brought unexpected connection or closeness?

Peace is my power. I return to it often.

"Joy is the simplest form of gratitude."
— Karl Barth

What moment this week brought me true joy?

What are 3 things I'm grateful for right now?

What 3 steps am I taking to set myself up for success?

What is my body or heart quietly asking for today?

What progress am I making that I haven't fully acknowledged?

Who do I want to connect with soon & why?

Every step I take is worthy of celebration.

"To be seen and loved is a human miracle."
— Sue Monk Kidd

What small joy felt like a big win for my heart?

What kind, loving words can I say to myself today?

What boundary or belief is keeping me grounded lately?

How can I care for myself through a rhythm or simple routine?

What have I received recently (help, love, feedback) that meant a lot?

What moment made me feel deeply seen or understood?

I nourish the real me—and she is more than enough.

"Speak the truth, even if your voice shakes."
— Maggie Kuhn

In what area of life do I currently feel the most confident?

What 3 things do I believe about God, or how God sees me?

What is something I could communicate more clearly going forward?

***1* Confidence & Truth-Telling**

What 3 things do I want more of in my day-to-day life?

I give myself a big high five for . . .

What small act or moment brought unexpected connection?

My confidence comes from being honest with myself.

"Celebrate every tiny victory—they add up."
— Unknown

When did I last feel truly confident & what helped create that feeling?

What's one value or truth I can embody more clearly this week?

What does God say about me & how does that speak to my situation?

What 3 things am I doing for my mental or emotional health?

What's worth celebrating in my life right now?

Where am I growing, even if the progress feels slow or messy?

I am growing stronger, even in the slow days.

What's one ordinary thing I deeply appreciated this week?

What affirmation or truth feels especially meaningful right now?

What 3 things am I doing to set myself up to win this season?

What are 3 things I long to see more of in the world?

What have I received, emotionally or practically, that touched me?

I felt like the most "me" version of myself when . . .

I live in alignment—and let joy follow.

"You are allowed to be both a masterpiece and a work in progress." — Sophia Bush

What activity or moment made me feel deeply loved this week?

What uplifting truth or affirmation will I carry with me this week?

What's something I did just for *me* this week?

***4* Love, Nourishment & Identity in Action**

What colorful, nourishing food did I enjoy lately & how did it feel?

My identity as a (mom/wife/sister/friend) really sparkled when . . .

What moment recently made me feel truly seen or celebrated?

Love flows when I show up as myself.

Checking in: Gathering the Gold

Which prompt or moment surprised me the most?

What has consistently brought me energy, peace, or clarity?

Where do I see signs of growth?

You may not know exactly what you want yet—but there are clues in what you miss, what you're drawn to, and what you daydream about.

One thing I want to protect more fiercely in my schedule:

One belief I want to practice living out loud:

One relationship or boundary I want to nurture:

This season I will live more . . .

**I am not the same woman who started this journal.
And that's the point.**

"The fullness of life is found in small moments of meaning." — Brené Brown

What experience or moment this week made me feel truly fulfilled?

What 3 beliefs do I hold about myself that feel true today?

What value or belief of mine could I live out more fully this week?

What is my heart or body quietly whispering (not shouting) to me?

What achievement deserves more recognition than I gave it?

What 3 chaotic things have I chosen lately & why?

I find fulfillment in the small, sacred moments.

"Your heart knows the way.
Run in that direction." — Rumi

What memory or thought is still warming my heart?

What does God say about me and how can I receive that truth?

What boundary / rule have I recently upheld, how did it serve me?

***2* Heart Smiles & Identity**

What 3 things do I crave more of in my daily life?

What personal identity stays steady, even when it all feels shaky?

What's stretching me right now & what is it making space for?

I listen to what brings warmth to my heart.

"Faith does not make things easy, it makes them possible." — Luke 1:37

Where am I feeling the most gratitude right now?

What mantra or phrase has been on repeat in my mind lately?

What belief do I want to practice with more intention this week?

***3* Spiritual Grounding & Accomplishment**

What 3 things am I doing to support my spiritual health?

What recent experience made me feel proud or accomplished?

When did I feel most "at home" this week & why or how?

I walk in quiet strength and faithful progress.

"Connection is why we're here; it gives purpose and meaning to our lives." — Brené Brown

What moment made me feel deeply connected this week?

What affirmation or mantra feels especially true for me right now?

What personal rule or rhythm can I follow to create calm?

What part of me feels tired, tight, or tender & what helps soothe it?

What can I celebrate today, big or small?

What moment recently made me feel fulfilled?

I welcome connection that nourishes my spirit.

What feeling have I experienced that I'd love to feel more often?

What part of my identity feels grounded and unshakable?

What "no" did I say recently that made space for something better?

What 3 things am I doing for my physical or mental health?

If describing a recent accomplishment in juicy detail, what would I say?

What's stretching me & what strength is it building in me?

I show up fully, not perfectly.

"Be still and know that I am God."
— Psalm 46:10

When did I feel most at peace & what was happening around me?

What are 3 things I'd love to see more of in the world?

What boundary or "no" helped me stay aligned with what matters?

What part of me feels worn out & what would replenish it?

What's something I handled recently that shows how far I've come?

What simple action brought unexpected connection or closeness?

Stillness reminds me who I am and who holds me.

"The joy we feel has little to do with the circumstances of our lives and everything to do with the focus of our lives." — Russell M. Nelson

What moment this week brought me true joy?

What are 3 things I'm grateful for right now?

What 3 steps am I taking to set myself up for success?

What is my body or heart quietly asking for today?

What progress am I making that I haven't fully acknowledged?

Who do I want to connect with soon & why?

I choose joy on purpose, not by accident.

"The most powerful relationship you will ever have is the relationship with yourself." — **Steve Maraboli**

What small joy felt like a big win for my heart?

What kind, loving words can I say to myself today?

What boundary or belief is keeping me grounded lately?

How can I care for myself through a rhythm or simple routine?

What have I received recently (help, love, feedback) that
    meant a lot?

What moment made me feel deeply seen or understood?

I give myself permission to be seen, known & nourished.

**"You can be scared and brave at the same time."
— Brené Brown**

In what area of life do I currently feel the most confident?

What 3 things do I believe about God, or how God sees me?

What is something I could communicate more clearly going forward?

What 3 things do I want more of in my day-to-day life?

I give myself a big high five for . . .

What small act or moment brought unexpected connection?

My truth is allowed to feel big & still belong.

When did I last feel truly confident & what helped create that feeling?

What's one value or truth I can embody more clearly this week?

What does God say about me & how does that speak to my situation?

2 Strength, Celebration & Growth

What 3 things am I doing for my mental or emotional health?

What's worth celebrating in my life right now?

Where am I growing, even if the progress feels slow or messy?

I'm proud of the strength I didn't know I had.

"Gratitude unlocks the fullness of life."
— Melody Beattie

What's one ordinary thing I deeply appreciated this week?

What affirmation or truth feels especially meaningful right now?

What 3 things am I doing to set myself up to win this season?

What are 3 things I long to see more of in the world?

What have I received, emotionally or practically, that touched me?

I felt like the most "me" version of myself when . . .

My life expands when I pause to appreciate.

"You are not required to set yourself on fire to keep others warm." — Unknown

What activity or moment made me feel deeply loved this week?

What uplifting truth or affirmation will I carry with me this week?

What's something I did just for *me* this week?

What colorful, nourishing food did I enjoy lately & how did it feel?

My identity as a (mom/wife/sister/friend) really sparkled when . . .

What moment recently made me feel truly seen or celebrated?

I tend to my needs with love, not guilt.

Checking in: Real Life, Real You

What part of life felt messy or unpredictable these last 12 weeks
   & how did I respond?

When did I stay true to myself in the middle of the mess?

Where did I adjust in a way that actually worked better for me?

**This check–in is about honoring how your real life
has shaped your rhythm and what you've learned
about navigating it as you.**

What's one rhythm I want to return to?

What's one habit or idea I need to release?

What new way of honoring my energy can I experiment with next?

This is the season where I give myself permission to . . .

**I give myself permission to thrive in real life,
not the imagined one.**

What experience or moment this week made me feel truly fulfilled?

What 3 beliefs do I hold about myself that feel true today?

What value or belief of mine could I live out more fully this week?

***1* Fulfillment & Self-Awareness**

What is my heart or body quietly whispering (not shouting) to me?

What achievement deserves more recognition than I gave it?

What 3 chaotic things have I chosen lately & why?

I nourish myself so I can show up whole.

What memory or thought is still warming my heart?

What does God say about me and how can I receive that truth?

What boundary / rule have I recently upheld, how did it serve me?

What 3 things do I crave more of in my daily life?

What personal identity stays steady, even when it all feels shaky?

What's stretching me right now & what is it making space for?

The way I love others starts with the way I love me.

"The best thing you can do is follow your joy."
— Oprah Winfrey

Where am I feeling the most gratitude right now?

What mantra or phrase has been on repeat in my mind lately?

What belief do I want to practice with more intention this week?

***3* Spiritual Grounding & Accomplishment**

What 3 things am I doing to support my spiritual health?

What recent experience made me feel proud or accomplished?

When did I feel most "at home" this week & why or how?

My joy matters & I'm allowed to chase it.

"Live your truth. Even if your voice shakes."
— Unknown

What moment made me feel deeply connected this week?

What affirmation or mantra feels especially true for me right now?

What personal rule or rhythm can I follow to create calm?

***4* Connection & Rest**

What part of me feels tired, tight, or tender & what helps soothe it?

What can I celebrate today, big or small?

What moment recently made me feel fulfilled?

My confidence grows when I walk in alignment.

What feeling have I experienced that I'd love to feel more often?

What part of my identity feels grounded and unshakable?

What "no" did I say recently that made space for something better?

What 3 things am I doing for my physical or mental health?

If describing a recent accomplishment in juicy detail, what would I say?

What's stretching me & what strength is it building in me?

Progress counts, even when it's quiet.

"You are enough just as you are."
— Meghan Markle

When did I feel most at peace & what was happening around me?

What are 3 things I'd love to see more of in the world?

What boundary or "no" helped me stay aligned with what matters?

What part of me feels worn out & what would replenish it?

What's something I handled recently that shows how far I've come?

What simple action brought unexpected connection or closeness?

I am not behind. I am becoming.

> **"What lies behind us and what lies before us are tiny matters compared to what lies within us."**
> **— Ralph Waldo Emerson**

What moment this week brought me true joy?

What are 3 things I'm grateful for right now?

What 3 steps am I taking to set myself up for success?

What is my body or heart quietly asking for today?

What progress am I making that I haven't fully acknowledged?

Who do I want to connect with soon & why?

There is strength in me I haven't met yet.

"Almost everything will work again if you unplug it for a few minutes... including you." — Anne Lamott

What small joy felt like a big win for my heart?

What kind, loving words can I say to myself today?

What boundary or belief is keeping me grounded lately?

***4* Nourishment & Being Seen**

How can I care for myself through a rhythm or simple routine?

What have I received recently (help, love, feedback) that meant a lot?

What moment made me feel deeply seen or understood?

My rest makes room for renewal.

"Faith is taking the first step even when you don't see the whole staircase."
— Martin Luther King Jr.

In what area of life do I currently feel the most confident?

What 3 things do I believe about God, or how God sees me?

What is something I could communicate more clearly going forward?

***1* Confidence & Truth-Telling**

What 3 things do I want more of in my day-to-day life?

I give myself a big high five for . . .

What small act or moment brought unexpected connection?

I take the next step with courage and calm.

"You are precious in my eyes, and honored, and I love you." — Isaiah 43:4

When did I last feel truly confident & what helped create that feeling?

What's one value or truth I can embody more clearly this week?

What does God say about me & how does that speak to my situation?

What 3 things am I doing for my mental or emotional health?

What's worth celebrating in my life right now?

Where am I growing, even if the progress feels slow or messy?

I carry divine worth into everything I do.

What's one ordinary thing I deeply appreciated this week?

What affirmation or truth feels especially meaningful right now?

What 3 things am I doing to set myself up to win this season?

What are 3 things I long to see more of in the world?

What have I received, emotionally or practically, that touched me?

I felt like the most "me" version of myself when . . .

I plan from identity, not urgency.

What activity or moment made me feel deeply loved this week?

What uplifting truth or affirmation will I carry with me this week?

What's something I did just for *me* this week?

What colorful, nourishing food did I enjoy lately & how did it feel?

My identity as a (mom/wife/sister/friend) really sparkled when . . .

What moment recently made me feel truly seen or celebrated?

I am worthy of restoration, not just recovery.

Checking in: Reclaim What's Yours

What part of me did I reconnect with or rediscover in the
  past 3 months?

What felt fake, forced, or not mine?

Where did I notice my intuition leading the way?

**This time, we are here to focus on reclaiming the
pieces of you that may have been buried under
busy-ness, pressure, or performance.**

One decision I'm proud I made:

One message I want to stop believing:

One core truth I want to live more boldly:

This is the season I embrace . . .

I am safe to walk in wholeness, not performance.

"Don't let the world make you hard."
— Kurt Vonnegut

What experience or moment this week made me feel truly fulfilled?

What 3 beliefs do I hold about myself that feel true today?

What value or belief of mine could I live out more fully this week?

What is my heart or body quietly whispering (not shouting) to me?

What achievement deserves more recognition than I gave it?

What 3 chaotic things have I chosen lately & why?

I protect my softness, it is strength.

"You have been assigned this mountain to show others it can be moved." — Unknown

What memory or thought is still warming my heart?

What does God say about me and how can I receive that truth?

What boundary / rule have I recently upheld, how did it serve me?

What 3 things do I crave more of in my daily life?

What personal identity stays steady, even when it all feels shaky?

What's stretching me right now & what is it making space for?

My story holds power and purpose.

Where am I feeling the most gratitude right now?

What mantra or phrase has been on repeat in my mind lately?

What belief do I want to practice with more intention this week?

***3* Spiritual Grounding & Accomplishment**

What 3 things am I doing to support my spiritual health?

What recent experience made me feel proud or accomplished?

When did I feel most "at home" this week & why or how?

I rise by staying rooted.

"To love and be loved is to feel the sun from both sides." — David Viscott

What moment made me feel deeply connected this week?

What affirmation or mantra feels especially true for me right now?

What personal rule or rhythm can I follow to create calm?

***4* Connection & Rest**

What part of me feels tired, tight, or tender & what helps soothe it?

What can I celebrate today, big or small?

What moment recently made me feel fulfilled?

Connection is my sunlight, I open to it.

"Life isn't about finding yourself. It's about creating yourself." — George Bernard Shaw

What feeling have I experienced that I'd love to feel more often?

What part of my identity feels grounded and unshakable?

What "no" did I say recently that made space for something better?

What 3 things am I doing for my physical or mental health?

If describing a recent accomplishment in juicy detail, what would I say?

What's stretching me & what strength is it building in me?

I am co-creating my life with intention.

When did I feel most at peace & what was happening around me?

What are 3 things I'd love to see more of in the world?

What boundary or "no" helped me stay aligned with what matters?

What part of me feels worn out & what would replenish it?

What's something I handled recently that shows how far I've come?

What simple action brought unexpected connection or closeness?

My honesty is healing, not harmful.

What moment this week brought me true joy?

What are 3 things I'm grateful for right now?

What 3 steps am I taking to set myself up for success?

***3* Joy, Progress & Planning**

What is my body or heart quietly asking for today?

What progress am I making that I haven't fully acknowledged?

Who do I want to connect with soon & why?

I honor my impact, even when it's unseen.

"Be patient with yourself, nothing in nature blooms all year." — Unknown

What small joy felt like a big win for my heart?

What kind, loving words can I say to myself today?

What boundary or belief is keeping me grounded lately?

***4* Nourishment & Being Seen**

How can I care for myself through a rhythm or simple routine?

What have I received recently (help, love, feedback) that
meant a lot?

What moment made me feel deeply seen or understood?

I bloom in rhythms, not deadlines.

"Happiness is not a goal... it's a by-product of a life well lived." — Eleanor Roosevelt

In what area of life do I currently feel the most confident?

What 3 things do I believe about God, or how God sees me?

What is something I could communicate more clearly going forward?

What 3 things do I want more of in my day-to-day life?

I give myself a big high five for . . .

What small act or moment brought unexpected connection?

I live well when I live true.

When did I last feel truly confident & what helped create that feeling?

What's one value or truth I can embody more clearly this week?

What does God say about me & how does that speak to my situation?

What 3 things am I doing for my mental or emotional health?

What's worth celebrating in my life right now?

Where am I growing, even if the progress feels slow or messy?

My light doesn't need permission.

"Be still and let your soul catch up." — Unknown

What's one ordinary thing I deeply appreciated this week?

What affirmation or truth feels especially meaningful right now?

What 3 things am I doing to set myself up to win this season?

What are 3 things I long to see more of in the world?

What have I received, emotionally or practically, that touched me?

I felt like the most "me" version of myself when . . .

I'm allowed to stop striving and simply be.

**"The soul always knows what to do to heal itself.
The challenge is to silence the mind."
— Caroline Myss**

What activity or moment made me feel deeply loved this week?

What uplifting truth or affirmation will I carry with me this week?

What's something I did just for *me* this week?

***4* Love, Nourishment & Identity in Action**

What colorful, nourishing food did I enjoy lately & how did it feel?

My identity as a (mom/wife/sister/friend) really sparkled when . . .

What moment recently made me feel truly seen or celebrated?

I let stillness speak louder than pressure.

Checking in: Fuel What Feeds You

What energized me, even when life was full?

What drained me, even when it looked important?

What rhythms supported both my health and my purpose?

Now it's time to strengthen what's working, and release what's draining. This checkpoint is a recalibration of your time, energy, and attention.

What do I want more of in the next 12 weeks?

What am I ready to say no to more easily?

Where do I need more support
   and what would asking for it look like?

In this season I fill myself with . . .

I nurture what nourishes me.

**"Don't shrink so others can be comfortable.
You're allowed to take up space." — Unknown**

What experience or moment this week made me feel truly fulfilled?

What 3 beliefs do I hold about myself that feel true today?

What value or belief of mine could I live out more fully this week?

***1* Fulfillment & Self-Awareness**

What is my heart or body quietly whispering (not shouting) to me?

What achievement deserves more recognition than I gave it?

What 3 chaotic things have I chosen lately & why?

I take up space with purpose and peace.

What memory or thought is still warming my heart?

What does God say about me and how can I receive that truth?

What boundary / rule have I recently upheld, how did it serve me?

What 3 things do I crave more of in my daily life?

What personal identity stays steady, even when it all feels shaky?

What's stretching me right now & what is it making space for?

I honor the woman I've rebuilt myself to be.

Where am I feeling the most gratitude right now?

What mantra or phrase has been on repeat in my mind lately?

What belief do I want to practice with more intention this week?

What 3 things am I doing to support my spiritual health?

What recent experience made me feel proud or accomplished?

When did I feel most "at home" this week & why or how?

I don't have to prove what's already true.

"Healing isn't about changing who you are, it's about letting go of who you are not." — Unknown

What moment made me feel deeply connected this week?

What affirmation or mantra feels especially true for me right now?

What personal rule or rhythm can I follow to create calm?

***4* Connection & Rest**

What part of me feels tired, tight, or tender & what helps soothe it?

What can I celebrate today, big or small?

What moment recently made me feel fulfilled?

I return to myself, gently and boldly.

"Let whatever you do today be enough."
— Unknown

What feeling have I experienced that I'd love to feel more often?

What part of my identity feels grounded and unshakable?

What "no" did I say recently that made space for something better?

***1* Confidence & Clarity**

What 3 things am I doing for my physical or mental health?

If describing a recent accomplishment in juicy detail, what would I say?

What's stretching me & what strength is it building in me?

Enough is not a benchmark... it's a birthright.

When did I feel most at peace & what was happening around me?

What are 3 things I'd love to see more of in the world?

What boundary or "no" helped me stay aligned with what matters?

What part of me feels worn out & what would replenish it?

What's something I handled recently that shows how far I've come?

What simple action brought unexpected connection or closeness?

Every season has sacred value.

"One day you will tell your story and it will become someone else's survival guide."
— Brené Brown

What moment this week brought me true joy?

What are 3 things I'm grateful for right now?

What 3 steps am I taking to set myself up for success?

What is my body or heart quietly asking for today?

What progress am I making that I haven't fully acknowledged?

Who do I want to connect with soon & why?

My story matters—even the messy middle.

What small joy felt like a big win for my heart?

What kind, loving words can I say to myself today?

What boundary or belief is keeping me grounded lately?

How can I care for myself through a rhythm or simple routine?

What have I received recently (help, love, feedback) that
   meant a lot?

What moment made me feel deeply seen or understood?

I show up soft and strong.

In what area of life do I currently feel the most confident?

What 3 things do I believe about God, or how God sees me?

What is something I could communicate more clearly going forward?

1 Confidence & Truth-Telling

What 3 things do I want more of in my day-to-day life?

I give myself a big high five for . . .

What small act or moment brought unexpected connection?

When I show up as myself, I shift the room.

When did I last feel truly confident & what helped create that feeling?

What's one value or truth I can embody more clearly this week?

What does God say about me & how does that speak to my situation?

What 3 things am I doing for my mental or emotional health?

What's worth celebrating in my life right now?

Where am I growing, even if the progress feels slow or messy?

My rest is radical & necessary.

What's one ordinary thing I deeply appreciated this week?

What affirmation or truth feels especially meaningful right now?

What 3 things am I doing to set myself up to win this season?

What are 3 things I long to see more of in the world?

What have I received, emotionally or practically, that touched me?

I felt like the most "me" version of myself when . . .

I speak to myself with reverence.

"It's okay to be a masterpiece and a work in progress at the same time." — Sophia Bush

What activity or moment made me feel deeply loved this week?

What uplifting truth or affirmation will I carry with me this week?

What's something I did just for *me* this week?

***4* Love, Nourishment & Identity in Action**

What colorful, nourishing food did I enjoy lately & how did it feel?

My identity as a (mom/wife/sister/friend) really sparkled when . . .

What moment recently made me feel truly seen or celebrated?

I am already worthy, even while becoming.

A Closing Letter,
Before Your Closing Words

Hey Beautiful, Confident, Resilient Friend,
This isn't a closing.
It's a return.

A return to the woman you've been gently uncovering, remembering, and becoming, one page and prompt at a time.

When you opened this journal, you may not have known where to begin.

Maybe all you had was a whisper that something inside you still mattered.

Something that had been quieted, pushed down, or buried beneath the noise of life.

But now? You've walked through something real.
This wasn't just 30 days or a year of writing prompts.
This was a rhythm. A retreat. A revival.

A quiet reclamation of
your confidence, your voice, your resilience.

And you didn't just survive it.
You showed up for it.
With your pen. With your heart. With your honesty.
In all your wholeness.

You're not the same woman you were when you took that leap of faith and invested your time * *and your hope* * into these pages.

Now, you hold something sacred in your hands:
A living document of who you are
and who you're becoming.

You may not have realized it at first, but you've been confidence stacking all along.

Every day, every page, every time you picked up your pen - you weren't just journaling.

You were remembering.
You were rebuilding.
You were rejoicing.
You were reconnecting.
You were reclaiming confidence from the inside out.

Not performative confidence. Not loud, forced, or polished.

But **rooted resilience**, *anchored* in your beliefs.

Affirmed by the mantras and truths you dared to speak over yourself.

Slowed enough to notice the beauty around you, even on the hard days.

Reminded of your strength, your past wins, and the way you always rise.

Gracious with yourself and your season as you paused to give thanks for what is and what's to come.

And **held** by your intentional choices and your sacred desires.

That's what this was all along:
A quiet, sacred return to the woman
you were always becoming.

Before you fully
close this journal,

Now, before you fully close this journal, I invite you to spend time with the **Final Recap Questions.**

These prompts are designed to help you see yourself clearly through the lens of the six confidence stacking pillars you've already been living.

You might be surprised how much has shifted.

And when you're ready * if you feel the nudge * there's more support waiting for you:

Not sure where to go next?
Download the 4 Anchors of Resilience Blueprint, a free mini companion to help you gently reset your days and move with intention.

Want to go deeper into the pillars?
Grab The Anchoring Amidst - Confidence Stacking Playbook for insight, reflection pages, and extra journal prompts to strengthen your growth.

Craving support and sisterhood?
The ISO Prosperity Sisterhood is open to you. Join our weekly live calls, sync your community to your vision, and walk in rhythm with women who get it.

* all here * - ***www.ShainaHargens.com/resources***

Choose your next step or simply linger here.
You're in charge. You make the rules.
And you're more than ready.

[find them all HERE]

A Final Prompt,
if your heart feels ready:

***Write a letter to yourself, dated 10 years from today.
Present tense. No rules. Just vision. Just truth. Just you.***

Let it pour.
Let it stretch.
Let it be full of details or completely open-ended.
    (I suggest a little of both)
If this feels foreign or hard, you're not alone. That's why I
keep a simple video training on it in the toolbox, ready
whenever you are - www.ShainaHargens.com/resources

You've done something remarkable, friend.

Not because it was big or flashy.
But because it was true.

You've returned to your confident, resilient, whole self.

This journal?
It's both your jumping-off point & your safe place to land.

Come back to it anytime.
Or start again with new ink, in a new season, returning to
you. **Again and again.**

Because resilience isn't something you find once.
It's something you stack, one honest, organic moment
that grows and stretches you at a time.

And you've already begun. The wheels are in motion.
With deep love and belief in your confident self.

XOXO *Shaina*

Final Recap: Rooted & Rising

What feels solid in me now that used to feel shaky?

How do I handle disruption or doubt differently than before?

What am I most proud of, even the stuff that no one else may see?

This cycle marks the culmination of a full spiral. You've gathered insights, reclaimed truth, and found rhythm. So… what's next in your becoming?

w e e k   o f : _ _ / _ _ / _ _

What version of me am I becoming?

What space does she need?

What support, structure, or softness does she thrive in?

In this season I become . . .

I am rooted in who I am,
and rising into who I'm becoming.

I am whole.
I am loved.
I am free.
I am me.